The
War
in the
Pacific

Peter Chrisp

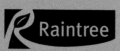

THE WORLD WARS

Published by Raintree Steck-Vaughn Publishers, an imprint of Steck-Vaughn Company.

Library of Congress Cataloging-in-Publication Data

Cataloging-in-publication data is available at the Library of Congress.

ISBN 0-7398-6063-1

Printed in Italy. Bound in the United States.
1 2 3 4 5 6 7 8 9 0 LB 07 06 05 04 03

Picture Acknowledgements
AKG 7, 9, 10-11, 19, 28, 38, 40, 45, 57; Black Star 31; Corbis 53, 59; Hodder Wayland Picture Library 13, 55; Hulton Getty 17; Peter Newark Historical Pictures 8; Peter Newark Military Pictures
4-5, 12, 16, 22, 23, 25, 27, 32, 35, 39, 41, 42, 43, 46-47, 49, 52, 54; Popperfoto 6, 15 (bottom), 21, 47, 50, 56; Topham Picturepoint 14-15, 51; TRH 58-59.

√ 11/17/05
√9/8/08

Contents

On Sunday, December 7, 1941, the sun rose in a beautiful blue sky above the islands of Hawaii, in the middle of the Pacific Ocean. For the U.S. Pacific fleet, based at Pearl Harbor on the island of Oahu, it was a day of rest. On board seventy ships, sailors were waking up, eating breakfast, or writing letters home.

Army private George Elliot was one of the few servicemen working that morning. He was operating the radar, the system of spotting distant objects with radio waves. At 7:02 A.M., Elliot noticed something unexpected on his radar screen—a mass of green dots, heading toward Hawaii from the north. This could only mean a large number of planes. Elliot phoned headquarters with the news, but was told to "forget it." The planes must be American bombers, expected to arrive that morning from the United States.

In fact, the dots on the radar screen were almost two hundred Japanese bomber and fighter planes. Although Japan and the United States were not at war, the Japanese had decided to launch a surprise attack on Pearl Harbor and destroy the U.S. Pacific fleet. Captain Mitsuo Fuchida led the first wave of planes, which reached Pearl Harbor at about 7:40 A.M. He was delighted to see that all the U.S. fighter planes were still on the ground. This meant that the Japanese had achieved total surprise. Fuchida gave the order to attack and led his planes swooping down toward the eight great battleships lined up next to each other in "Battleship Row."

"Like a Hurricane"

Mitsuo Fuchida later described his feelings as he attacked Pearl Harbor:

"Like a hurricane out of nowhere, my torpedo planes, dive-bombers, and fighters struck suddenly with indescribable fury. As smoke began to billow and the proud battleships, one by one started tilting, my heart was almost ablaze with joy."

Quoted in "Pearl Harbor to Calvary," *Christian History* magazine

For two hours, the Japanese bombed the ships, docks, and airfields of Pearl Harbor. At the end, 18 ships were sunk or badly damaged, 188 planes had been destroyed, and 2,335 servicemen and 69 civilians were dead. It took two weeks before all the fires on the burning ships were put out.

The next day, Admiral William "Bull" Halsey gazed in fury and horror at the smoking wreckage of his fleet. He said, "By the time we're finished with them, Japanese will be spoken only in hell!" In fact, the damage could have been much worse. The Japanese had failed to destroy the dry docks, ammunition stores, and fuel installations. The U.S. aircraft carriers, away from Hawaii at the time, had also escaped.

The Pacific War

This attack was the beginning of the Pacific War, the largest naval conflict in history. For almost four years, the United States and its allies fought the Japanese across vast stretches of the world's greatest ocean, the Pacific, a name that means "peaceful." The war was fought in many different climates and landscapes, from the steamy jungles of Guadalcanal in the south to the icy Aleutian Islands in the north. Fighting also took many forms. There were seaborne invasions of islands, great battles between fleets of aircraft carriers, submarine attacks on ships, fire raids on cities, and the first, and so far only, use of atomic bombs.

Hit by nine torpedoes, the battleship West Virginia *sinks, billowing smoke. Behind it lies the* Tennessee, *struck by two bombs. Both were later repaired, and went out to battle the Japanese again.*

CHAPTER TWO

Why War Came

Japan is made up of a group of islands whose total size is about the same as the state of California. To understand why this little island nation attacked the United States, the world's most powerful nation, we need to look back at Japanese history.

God-Emperor

Japan has had the same royal family for more than two thousand years. The emperor was believed to be descended from the Sun Goddess, Amaterasu, so no other family could take over the royal line. Descended from a god, the emperor was thought to be a god himself. Every morning and evening, people prayed in front of his portrait. Children were told that they would be struck blind if they looked at his face. The belief that they were ruled by a god made the Japanese feel superior to all other nations. They were also proud of the fact that they had never lost a war or been successfully invaded.

Emperor Hirohito (1901–89)

Emperor Hirohito became Japan's emperor in 1926. He was passionate about marine (ocean) science and his happiest times were spent in his laboratory, studying underwater life. Hirohito had been trained since childhood to believe that his job was "to reign but not rule." He had to approve all decisions made by his government, but he was not expected to make any political decisions himself. He represented the whole nation, so he could not take sides in politics.

As a sign of respect, no Japanese person ever used Hirohito's name. While he lived they referred to him simply as the "Tenno" (emperor). After his death he became known as the "Showa Emperor," from the title he had given his reign— Showa meaning "Enlightened Peace." Hirohito wanted to be remembered as a man of peace.

Emperor Hirohito had to wear dress uniform and ride a white horse for formal photographs. In fact, he was much happier wearing a shabby old suit.

Western Empires

In the 19th century, Western powers—Great Britain, the United States, the Netherlands, Russia, and France—all seized territory in Asia and the Pacific. The Japanese found themselves surrounded by powerful "European empires." They both feared and admired the westerners. Unlike other Asian peoples, they copied Western methods—building factories, railroads, and a large army and navy. Between 1868 and the early 1900s, Japan was transformed into a modern industrial nation.

The Japanese wanted to be treated as equals by the Western powers and, like them, to conquer their own lands overseas. Between 1894 and 1910, Japan's army conquered the island of Formosa (Taiwan), Korea, and Southern Manchuria. This was the beginning of a Japanese empire.

Trading Nation

Japan has a shortage of raw materials, such as oil, coal, iron, and rubber. In order to build Japanese industries, all these materials had to be imported from abroad. They were paid for with goods produced in the new factories, such as silk and cotton cloth. Japan became a trading nation, with Japanese merchant ships sailing the world's oceans. The growth of trade and industry led to a swift rise in the Japanese population, as more jobs and money meant that people could afford to have bigger families. Between 1873 and 1934, the population rose from 35 to 65 million people. For the first time ever, Japan had to import food for its people.

The Japanese called their country Nippon, "the land of the rising sun." The rising sun flag carried by the military also stood for the emperor, descended from the sun goddess.

World Crisis

In 1929 there was a worldwide economic crisis with a tremendous fall in international trading. The "Great Depression" that followed resulted in unemployment and poverty for millions of people. The crisis meant that Japan was suddenly robbed of its overseas markets. The country could no longer sell goods abroad or afford to import raw materials and food.

Dealing with the Depression

Different countries found different ways of dealing with the Depression. In the United States in 1932, Franklin Delano Roosevelt was elected president after promising a "New Deal" for the American people. Roosevelt used the power of the government to help the 14 million unemployed people with food and money. He also organized major building projects to provide work.

In other countries, the crisis led to a loss of faith in democracy—rule by parties elected by the people. In 1933 Adolf Hitler, leader of the Nazi Party, made himself dictator (absolute ruler) of Germany, banning all other political parties. Hitler's solution to Germany's unemployment was to build up its armed forces and to threaten his neighbors with war. He put the unemployed to work in arms factories and introduced compulsory military service for men.

In 1933 in the depths of the Depression, unemployed Americans line up for free soup, coffee, and donuts.

Japan's Answer

Like Adolf Hitler, many Japanese people thought that the answer to their problems lay in warfare. The conquest of the Chinese province of Manchuria, rich in coal and iron, would provide a new source of raw materials. Japanese people could also settle in Manchuria and farm the land there. This would solve Japan's overpopulation problem and provide food for the home islands.

Japan had already conquered part of Manchuria and had an army there, in Kwantung. In 1931 a group of officers of the Kwantung Army decided, on their own initiative, to start a war. To provide a reason, they blew up part of a railway line, blaming the attack on the Chinese. The Kwantung Army then launched a full-scale invasion of Manchuria. The invasion had not been approved by the emperor or his government. Hirohito and many of his ministers were furious but felt powerless to do anything about it. Government promises to withdraw from Manchuria were simply ignored by the Kwantung Army. By the end of 1931, Manchuria had been conquered, and the Kwantung Army set up its own government there.

Patriotic Societies

The easy conquest of Manchuria was greeted with great excitement in Japan. Many military officers and students joined secret "superpatriotic" organizations, such as the "Cherry Blossom Society." They talked of further Japanese conquests. Japan's Prime Minister, Tsuyoshi Inukai, had refused to recognize the Kwantung Army government of Manchuria. On May 14, 1932, he was shot dead by a group of naval officers from the Cherry Blossom Society. Although the killers were caught, they were given only light sentences. Many Japanese people were on their side. The War Minister, General Sadao Araki, said that they had acted "in the genuine belief that it would be good for the Empire."

In January 1932, after conquering Manchuria, the Japanese attacked the Chinese port of Shanghai. The Chinese soldiers, shown here, successfully held off the attack.

Militarists Take Power

Little by little, Japan was being taken over by militarists who wanted to expand the army and spread military values such as discipline and the glorification of war. Any politician who tried to stand up to them risked being assassinated. Japanese rule in the 1930s was later described as "government by assassination." In September 1932 the Japanese government gave in to the militarists and officially recognized the conquest of Manchuria. Japan was condemned by the League of Nations —the grouping of countries set up in 1920 to promote world peace. Furious at being criticized, the Japanese left the League.

Group Loyalty

Unlike Western societies, which place a high value on individual freedom, Japanese people have always put loyalty to a group before their own wishes. This group might be their family, their village, or their fellow workers. To the Japanese, Western individualism can sometimes appear to be the same as selfishness. This Japanese willingness to unite for a common purpose was a great help to the militarists in taking over the country in the 1930s.

Attacking China

In July 1937 Japan launched a new full-scale war on China. The Japanese army swept into eastern China and, after months of fierce fighting, captured the Chinese capital, Nanking. In Nanking the Japanese soldiers went on the rampage, brutally killing more than 300,000 Chinese civilians. Despite losing their capital city, the Chinese fought back fiercely. Their leader, Chiang Kai-Shek, was greatly helped by the United States and Britain, which sent supplies to his army through Burma. Consequently, the Japanese began to see the Western democracies as their enemies. At the same time in Europe, Adolf Hitler was using the threat of war to seize territory. The European democracies of Britain and France were anxious to preserve peace but unwilling to become involved. It was only when Germany invaded Czechoslovakia in 1938 that the British and French decided that Hitler had to be stopped. When he invaded Poland, on September 1, 1939, they declared war on Germany. World War II had begun.

Roosevelt Acts

U.S. President Franklin D. Roosevelt sent arms and supplies to help the British, who fought alone against Hitler after France fell to the Germans in May 1940. He also put pressure on the Japanese to withdraw from China, banning the export of many goods to Japan. Roosevelt wanted to stop the Germans and the Japanese, but he knew that U.S. citizens did not want to fight a war. Campaigning for reelection in 1940, the president made a promise: "Your boys are not going to be sent into any foreign war." Such statements encouraged the Japanese to see the United States as a weak nation.

"Americans are Weak"

Nogi Harumichi, a young Japanese university student in 1940, described what he was told about American democracy:

"'Democracy' meant you could do whatever you pleased. If we found ourselves where we had to fight America, we were assured we would not have to worry. America was a democratic nation...they can't unite for a common purpose. One blow against them and they'll fall to pieces."

Quoted in Haruko and Theodore Cook, *Japan at War: An Oral History*

Japanese soldiers celebrate their capture of a Chinese artillery camp in the summer of 1937.

Roosevelt Cuts Off Japan's Oil

For the Japanese, Germany's conquest of France in May 1940 provided a wonderful opportunity. It meant that they could invade French Indochina without having to fight a war against France. The Japanese could then use Indochina, on the border of China, as a base to finish their war against the Chinese. In September 1940, Japan allied with Germany and, with Hitler's approval, the Japanese army occupied Indochina.

President Roosevelt reacted by banning the export of iron and steel to Japan and by beginning a massive buildup of the U.S. armed forces. In July 1941 he cut off the supply of oil to Japan. Roosevelt demanded a Japanese withdrawal from Indochina and China, something to which no Japanese leader could agree. Yet without oil, the Japanese could not go on fighting the Chinese for long. They had to convince Roosevelt to change his policies or find a new source of oil. The only other source of oil lay in the Dutch East Indies, south of British territory in Malaya (present-day Malaysia) and the U.S.-controlled Philippines. To get to the Dutch East Indies, the Japanese would first have to fight the British and the Americans.

For months the Japanese leaders negotiated with Roosevelt without success. They decided that if he would not back down by November 25, 1941, they would go to war.

General Hideki Tojo, the Japanese Prime Minister, was short-tempered, and was nicknamed "Razor Tojo," because of his sharp tongue.

General Hideki Tojo (1884–1948)

Japan's Prime Minister from October 1941 to July 1944 was General Hideki Tojo, a leading militarist. Tojo had risen to the top through hard work and determination. He believed that nothing was impossible, given a single-minded will to succeed. Tojo placed great faith in the Japanese "fighting spirit." This was enough, he believed, to beat even a country as powerful as the United States.

They could not afford to wait any longer; Japan was growing weaker while the United States was becoming stronger and stronger.

Yamamoto's Plan

Admiral Isoroku Yamamoto had lived in the United States and knew that the Americans were too powerful for a country the size of Japan to defeat. Yet once the decision for war had been made, it was Yamamoto's responsibility to work out a plan. He believed that Japan's only chance was to launch a surprise attack, destroying the U.S. fleet at Pearl Harbor. At the same time, Japan would attack the British Army in Malaya and the U.S. Army in the Philippines.

The Admiral warned that if his plan succeeded, it would allow him "to run wild considerably for the first six months or a year" but he had "utterly no confidence for the second and third years." It would then be up to the Japanese leaders to make peace with the United States. General Tojo believed that the United States would agree to peace. He said, "If we are fair in governing the occupied areas, attitudes toward us would probably relax. America may be enraged for a while, but she will later come to understand."

From a military point of view, Yamamoto's plan worked. On December 7, 1941, the U.S. fleet was largely destroyed at Pearl Harbor. From any other point of view, it was a disastrous failure. It united every American in bitter hatred of Japan. On December 11, 1941, Adolf Hitler declared war on the United States. America was now forced to fight two wars, one in Europe and one in the Pacific.

Two wrecked destroyers, photographed soon after the attack, lie in one of the dry docks of Pearl Harbor. The Japanese underestimated the impact that the bombing would have on the American view of Japan.

CHAPTER THREE

Japanese Conquests

Malaya and Singapore

A few hours before the attack on Pearl Harbor, 70,000 Japanese soldiers under Lieutenant General Tomoyuki Yamashita landed in British Malaya. Their goal was the great British naval base on the island of Singapore, at Malaya's southern tip. Yamashita's soldiers swept south through the jungle, many on bicycles. In Malaya, the British and their allies found themselves under attack from the air, the sea, and the land. They retreated to Singapore.

To Britain, Singapore was much more than just a naval base. The port, which had been British since 1819, was a symbol of the empire and the power of the British Navy. It was defended by huge, powerful guns, an army of 85,000 British, Australian, and Indian soldiers, and a fleet of warships.

The Prince of Wales, *with 175 antiaircraft guns, was the best-armed battleship in the British Navy. Its sinking was a terrible shock to the British government.*

Sinking the Fleet

When news of the invasion of Malaya reached Singapore, the British fleet sailed out to attack the Japanese Navy. The fleet was made up of the great battleship *Prince of Wales,* the battle cruiser *Repulse,* and four destroyers. The Japanese were ready for them. On December 10, a force of 85 torpedo-bomber planes attacked the British fleet, sinking both the *Prince of Wales* and the *Repulse* in less than three hours. This was the first time that large warships had ever been sunk in the open ocean by planes. The sinking showed that the age of the battleship, which had ruled the seas for four hundred years, was over. Victory in the Pacific War would depend on air power.

Japanese stand guard over British prisoners in Singapore. The Japanese could not believe how easy the capture of the city had been.

Pointing the Wrong Way

Singapore had a fatal weakness. Its great guns, which pointed out to sea, were armed with shells designed to sink ships. They were of no use against swarms of Japanese infantry riding bicycles. There was no defense against an attack from the land, as it was thought that the thick Malayan jungle would stop an army from trying to come this way. British Prime Minister Winston Churchill was horrified when he was told this. He wrote, "The possibility of Singapore having no landward defenses no more entered my mind than that of a battleship being launched without a bottom." On February 10, 1942, Churchill sent a desperate order to General Archibald Percival, commander in Singapore: "Battle must be fought to the bitter end. Commanders and senior officers should die with their troops. The honor of the British Empire is at stake."

Yamashita's Bluff

By the time the Japanese reached Singapore, they were almost out of ammunition, and outnumbered by an army three times bigger. Yet Yamashita fooled General Percival into believing that he could capture the city. When the two met on February 15, Yamashita demanded an immediate British surrender. He said that if Percival refused, he would invade the city that very night. Despite Churchill's order to fight "to the bitter end," Percival surrendered because he knew that the morale, or fighting spirit, of his men had broken down. Yamashita later described his strategy as "a bluff, a bluff that worked." He said, "I felt that if we had to fight in the city we would be beaten."

As Churchill predicted, the fall of Singapore was a shattering blow to the British Empire in Asia. The Japanese forced their prisoners to sweep the streets of the city. From such a humiliation the British Empire would never recover.

The Philippines

On the day of the Pearl Harbor attack and the invasion of Malaya, a third Japanese campaign began in the Philippines. These islands, governed by the United States since 1898, had recently been granted independence, to come into effect in 1946. They were defended by a large U.S. and Filipino army, commanded by the most famous American general, Douglas MacArthur. Unlike the British in Singapore, MacArthur had a strong air force, including 35 new B-17 bomber planes. Army chief General George Marshall had boasted that these planes, nicknamed "flying fortresses," were the "greatest concentration of heavy bomber strength anywhere in the world."

Invasion

News of the Pearl Harbor raid reached MacArthur eight hours before his own forces came under attack. Yet, for unknown reasons, MacArthur did not act. When the Japanese bombers arrived, they found all the U.S. planes still on the ground. Within a few hours, the whole of MacArthur's air force was destroyed. With no air force, it was now impossible to stop the Japanese invasion of the islands, which followed soon, on December 10. MacArthur's troops were forced to

General Douglas MacArthur (1880-1964)

General MacArthur commanded the U.S. Army in the Far East. Before the war he spent several years in the Philippines, helping the islands build up their armed forces in preparation for independence. MacArthur believed himself to be a great man who would be remembered alongside the other famous generals of history. He liked appearing in the newspapers and went out of his way to look like a great general. The public loved him, but President Roosevelt and the other U.S. commanders found him hard to deal with. They saw him as a vain man who put his public image before everything else.

Douglas MacArthur was usually photographed wearing a hat covered with gold braid that he had designed himself. Like his corncob pipe, this made him instantly recognizable to the U.S. public.

In April 1942, MacArthur's U.S. and Filipino soldiers surrender in Bataan. Few of these men would survive almost three years as prisoners of the Japanese.

retreat down a 25-mile (40-km)-long peninsula (arm of land) called Bataan.

In Bataan, the U.S. army held out bravely for four months against the Japanese. As food ran out, the men ate horses, monkeys, and snakes. When it was clear that they would soon have to surrender, Roosevelt ordered MacArthur to leave for Australia. He did not want his most famous general to be captured by the Japanese. On March 11, MacArthur left the Philippines, promising his men that he would return with a new army to rescue them. The following month, the army in Bataan surrendered.

Worst Defeat in History

The attack on Pearl Harbor had been a "hit and run" raid. The ships could be repaired or replaced. The loss of the Philippines, with its army of 78,000 men, was much more serious. It was the worst U.S. defeat in history. Yet, unlike the commanders at Pearl Harbor, MacArthur did not lose his job over his failure in the Philippines. He was popular in the United States, and Roosevelt knew that at this dark time the public needed heroes. Newspaper headlines described MacArthur as the "Hero of the Pacific." His promise to his men, "I shall return" became a rallying cry for the Pacific War.

Easy Victories

In the opening campaigns of the Pacific War, the Japanese were triumphant everywhere. By April 1942, they had conquered the Philippines, Malaya, Singapore, Hong Kong, and the Dutch East Indies. They were also advancing through Burma in the west of Asia and New Guinea in the South Pacific. The Japanese leaders had not, however, foreseen one result of their easy victories. They now had many thousands of prisoners to deal with.

The countries invaded and occupied by Japan between December 1941 and August 1942.

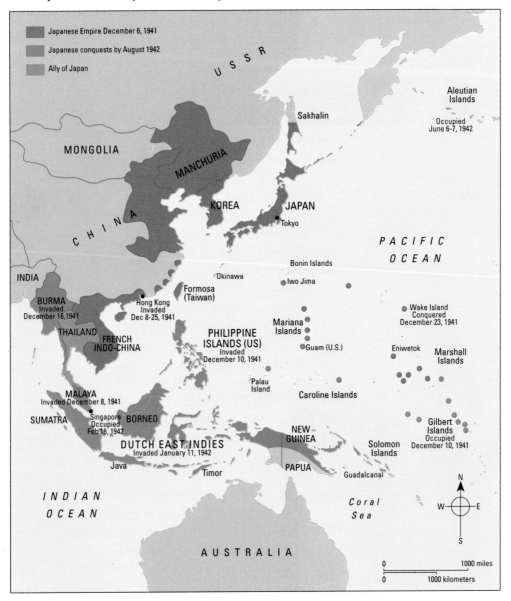

Japanese Empire December 6, 1941

Japanese conquests by August 1942

Ally of Japan

USSR

MONGOLIA

MANCHURIA

KOREA

CHINA

JAPAN
Tokyo

Sakhalin

Aleutian
Islands

Occupied
June 6-7, 1942

PACIFIC
OCEAN

Bonin Islands

INDIA

Okinawa

Iwo Jima

BURMA
Invaded
December 16, 1941

Hong Kong
Invaded
Dec 8-25, 1941

Formosa
(Taiwan)

Wake Island
Conquered
December 23, 1941

THAILAND

FRENCH
INDO-CHINA

PHILIPPINE
ISLANDS (US)
Invaded
December 10, 1941

Mariana
Islands

Guam (U.S.)

Eniwetok

Marshall
Islands

MALAYA
Invaded December 8, 1941

Palau
Island

Caroline Islands

SUMATRA

Singapore
Occupied
Feb 16, 1942

BORNEO

NEW
GUINEA

Solomon
Islands

Gilbert
Islands
Occupied
December 10, 1941

DUTCH EAST INDIES
Invaded January 11, 1942

Java

Timor

PAPUA

Guadalcanal

INDIAN
OCEAN

Coral
Sea

AUSTRALIA

N
W—E
S

0   1000 miles
0   1000 kilometers

Death March

In the Philippines, the Japanese took 12,000 American and 66,000 Filipino prisoners. The prisoners were ordered to march 62 miles (100 km) from Bataan to a railroad station, to be taken by train to a prison camp. This was an easy two-day march for Japanese soldiers, but it took the prisoners twice as long. They were already half-starved after months in Bataan, and many were also wounded or sick with malaria and dysentery.

The journey would be remembered as the "Bataan Death March." Without food or water, many prisoners collapsed in the scorching sun. The Japanese guards, frustrated at their slow pace, beat and killed their prisoners. One survivor, Anton Bilek, recalled, "'If you fell to the side, you were either shot by the guards or you were bayoneted and left there." About 700 Americans and 10,000 Filipinos died on the Bataan Death March.

Exhausted and hungry American and Filipino prisoners take a short rest on the Bataan Death March. The prisoner on the right looks up warily at the standing Japanese guard.

Railroad of Death

Many of the prisoners captured in Singapore and the Dutch East Indies were forced to build a 400-mile (640-km) railroad linking Siam (Thailand) with Burma. The working conditions were terrible. A quarter of the 60,000 prisoners died from disease, lack of food, and beatings by the guards.

Why Were They So Cruel?

The Japanese had no sympathy for prisoners. They had been taught that it was every soldier's duty to die before surrendering. Abe Hiroshi, an engineer on the Burma-Siam railroad, remembered, "For us Japanese, becoming a prisoner was itself the greatest shame imaginable—the same as death." Japanese military training encouraged cruelty. Constantly beaten by their officers, many soldiers took the chance to beat and kill others in turn.

Men Into Demons

Tominaga Shozu, an officer who trained new recruits in China, described his methods:

"As the last stage of their training, we made them bayonet living human beings ....Prisoners were blindfolded and tied to poles. The soldiers dashed forward to bayonet their target at the shout of 'Charge!' Some stopped on the way. We kicked them and made them do it. After that, a man could do anything easily ....Everyone became a demon within three months."

Quoted in Haruko and Theodore Cook, *Japan at War: An Oral History*

CHAPTER FOUR

Striking Back

The winter of 1941–42 was a depressing time in the United States, because the only stories in the news were of allied defeats. President Roosevelt, desperate to give the public some good news, asked his military leaders to organize a bombing raid on Japan. This would be a way of avenging the attack on Pearl Harbor.

The Doolittle Raid

In April 1942 two U.S. aircraft carriers, the *Hornet* and the *Enterprise,* headed across the Pacific, toward Japan. On board the *Hornet* were sixteen B-25 bomber planes from the Army Air Force. The flying crews were commanded by Lieutenant-Colonel James Doolittle, thought to be the army's most skilled pilot. The plan was for the planes to bomb Japanese war factories and ships and then fly onward to land in friendly territory in China. However, during the night of April 17, the ships were spotted by a Japanese patrol boat. Although this boat was sunk, it had had time to send a warning message to Japan. Doolittle decided that he had to take off at once, even though he was 150 miles (240 km) from his planned launch point. This meant that his pilots might not have enough fuel to reach safety in China.

On April 18, at 7:20 A.M., the pilots climbed into their planes. There was a strong wind and a rough sea, and this was the first time that any of them had taken off from the rolling deck of a ship. Despite the weather, they all managed to get in the air. Soon after midday, the bombers appeared over Tokyo. Children watching from playgrounds below waved up at them, thinking they were Japanese planes putting on a show. Then the bombs began to fall and explosions shook the city.

The bombers missed most of their military targets, though they destroyed about 90 buildings and killed 50 civilians. They then flew on eastward, just reaching the

On the deck of the Hornet, *in front of a B-25 bomber plane, Admiral "Bull" Halsey (right) shares a joke with Lieutenant Colonel James Doolittle. Soon Doolittle and his bombers would be flying toward Tokyo.*

Chinese coast. Three men died in crash landings, and eight others were captured by the Japanese. The rest eventually reached safety.

Sentenced to Death

The eight captured pilots were put on trial in China and sentenced to death as war criminals. On October 15, 1942, Harold Spatz, William Farrow, and Dean Hallmark were shot. The emperor then reduced the sentences of the rest to life imprisonment. The execution of the three pilots was publicly announced, in order to discourage the United States from launching further bombing raids on Japan. In fact, it only served to cause outrage in the United States. This showed the shortsightedness of Japan's military leaders. They had started a war against the most powerful nation on earth, with no long-term plan for ending it. The Japanese generals knew that the fighting would only end when the United States agreed to make peace, but the killing of the pilots, like the attack on Pearl Harbor, united every U.S. citizen in bitter hatred of the Japanese.

Some survivors of Doolittle's raid pose with their Chinese rescuers.

"You Asked For It!"

The Purple Heart, a U.S. film of 1944, dealt with the fate of the captured Doolittle pilots. During the trial scene, one of the pilots makes a speech:

"You can kill us—all of us, or part of us. But if you think that's going to put the fear of God into the United States of America and stop them from sending other fliers to bomb you, you're wrong, dead wrong. They'll blacken your skies and burn your cities to the ground.... This is your war. You wanted it. You asked for it. And now you're going to get it. And it won't be finished until your dirty little empire is wiped off the face of the earth!"

Although these words were written by a screenwriter, they sum up how many Americans felt about the Japanese.

Losing Face

Although the Doolittle raid had done little military damage, it came as a terrible shock to the Japanese leaders. They had been at war in China for eleven years, yet this was the first time that Japan had ever been bombed. The generals and admirals had assured the emperor that the country was safe, and they felt great shame that they had allowed the raid to happen. They had "lost face." On board his ship, Admiral Yamamoto was so upset that he retired to his cabin for a day, refusing to speak to anyone.

Yamamoto's New Plan

For weeks, Yamamoto had been pressing for a naval invasion of the U.S. base at Midway, right in the middle of the Pacific Ocean. Yamamoto wanted to draw what was left of the U.S. fleet into a final battle. Once the fleet was destroyed, the Japanese could use Midway to threaten Hawaii and the West Coast of the United States. Then the Americans would be forced to make peace.

Yamamoto's plan was opposed by the generals and the other admirals, who argued that Midway was too far away from Japan to be supplied or defended. They believed that the place to finish off the U.S. fleet was in the South Pacific, where the Japanese could use the Solomon Islands as bases to help win the battle. When Yamamoto eventually came out of his cabin, he demanded that his plan be adopted. After the Doolittle raid, he declared, it was a matter of honor to capture Midway to stop future raids on Japan. All the military leaders now agreed with Yamamoto.

In calling for the bombing of Japan, Roosevelt had only meant to cheer up the U.S. public. Without realizing it, he had managed to change Japanese military planning. The resulting Battle of Midway would alter the whole course of the Pacific War.

Admiral Yamamoto consulting a map. He saw the Doolittle raid as a personal defeat. By allowing the United States to launch an attack on Tokyo, he had failed in his most sacred duty: to protect the emperor.

CHAPTER FIVE

The Battle of Midway

Admiral Yamamoto knew that one key part of his Pearl Harbor attack had failed. Three U.S. aircraft carriers, the *Saratoga,* the *Lexington,* and the *Enterprise,* had escaped, as they had been out at sea during the attack. Early in 1942, they were joined by two other carriers, the *Hornet* and the *Yorktown* (see panel) from the United States. Yamamoto's plan for the Battle of Midway was to catch and sink these ships. As long as the U.S. carrier fleet sailed the Pacific, Japan would not be safe.

Planning Midway

Admiral Yamamoto assembled a huge fleet including 11 battleships, 8 aircraft carriers, 65 destroyers, 22 cruisers, and 18 submarines. He was confident of victory at Midway. To confuse his enemy, Yamamoto divided his forces into five groups, operating over more than 2,000 square miles (5,200 sq km) of ocean.

Aircraft Carriers

Developed in 1918 at the end of World War I, aircraft carriers are ships with wide, flat decks used for launching and recovering planes. Although several countries built carriers in the 1920s and 1930s, most naval leaders still believed that victory at sea depended on great battleships firing powerful guns at each other. Admiral Yamamoto was one of the few people who understood that air power had changed the way sea battles would be fought.

The first aircraft-carrier battle in history took place between the Japanese and American navies on May 4–8, 1942, in the Coral Sea northwest of Australia. This was a new kind of battle, in which the rival fleets did not even come within sight of each other. The outcome depended entirely on aircraft searching for enemy ships. Neither side won. The Japanese planes sank the *Lexington* and badly damaged the *Yorktown,* while the Americans destroyed a Japanese carrier, the *Shoho,* and two other ships. Yet this was a great boost to the American fliers; the sinking of the *Shoho* was their first real success of the war.

Death of the *Shoho, a 1942 painting by the U.S. war artist Robert Benney, showing the most dramatic moment of the Battle of the Coral Sea. Attacked by U.S. bombers, the Japanese carrier,* Shoho, *is in flames.*

As part of his fleet raced toward Midway, another group of ships headed north toward the Aleutian Islands. Yamamoto wanted to make the Americans think that the Aleutians were the target, not Midway. He planned to repeat Pearl Harbor and spring another surprise.

On the American side, Admiral Chester Nimitz had 8 cruisers, 17 destroyers, and just 3 carriers, including the hastily repaired *Yorktown.* Although greatly outnumbered, the Americans had three advantages. They had the island of Midway, which meant that their pilots had somewhere to land even if their carriers were sunk. Unlike the Japanese they had radar, which would help them find the enemy planes. Most importantly, they had broken the Japanese naval codes—the secret signals used to send radio messages. This time Yamomoto would not be able to stage a surprise, because Admiral Nimitz knew when and where the attack was coming.

The Battle Begins

Before dawn on June 4, 1942, the Japanese striking force, commanded by Vice Admiral Chuichi Nagumo, headed toward Midway. He had four carriers, *Kaga* ("Increased Joy"), *Soryu* ("Green Dragon"), *Hiryu* ("Flying Dragon"), and *Akagi* ("Red Castle"). The Americans knew that the attack was coming, so search planes from Midway were in the air before dawn, on the lookout for the Japanese. At 5:34 A.M., one of the U.S. planes found the enemy fleet and radioed the news to Admiral Nimitz. He ordered the land-based bombers at Midway: "Go all out for the carriers."

Soon after, U.S. radar picked up 108 Japanese planes heading toward Midway. While the Midway bombers took off to attack the carriers, the fighter planes went into action against the incoming planes. The American fighter pilots were outnumbered, and were no match for the Japanese in their faster planes. Seventeen U.S. planes were shot down and seven others badly damaged. The American attack on the carriers was just as ineffective, with all the bombers missing their targets.

The Battle of Midway.

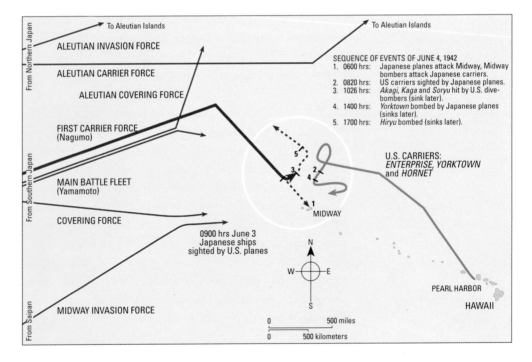

From Northern Japan

To Aleutian Islands

ALEUTIAN INVASION FORCE

ALEUTIAN CARRIER FORCE

ALEUTIAN COVERING FORCE

FIRST CARRIER FORCE (Nagumo)

From Southern Japan

MAIN BATTLE FLEET (Yamamoto)

COVERING FORCE

0900 hrs June 3 Japanese ships sighted by U.S. planes

From Saipan

MIDWAY INVASION FORCE

To Aleutian Islands

SEQUENCE OF EVENTS OF JUNE 4, 1942
1. 0600 hrs: Japanese planes attack Midway, Midway bombers attack Japanese carriers.
2. 0820 hrs: US carriers sighted by Japanese planes.
3. 1026 hrs: *Akagi, Kaga* and *Soryu* hit by U.S. dive-bombers (sink later).
4. 1400 hrs: *Yorktown* bombed by Japanese planes (sinks later).
5. 1700 hrs: *Hiryu* bombed (sinks later).

U.S. CARRIERS: *ENTERPRISE, YORKTOWN* and *HORNET*

MIDWAY

N
W — E
S

PEARL HARBOR

HAWAII

0 — 500 miles
0 — 500 kilometers

The Carrier Battle

Unknown to Nagumo, the U.S. carrier force of the *Enterprise,* the *Hornet,* and the *Yorktown* had been waiting northeast of Midway and was now heading toward him. From 9:30 to 10:24 A.M., three waves of U.S. torpedo-bombers launched from these ships attacked the Japanese carriers. These attacks also failed, with 35 of the 41 bombers shot down. At 10:24 A.M., Nagumo was sure he had won the battle. He had beaten off four attacks, and now he was ready to launch his own counterattack on the U.S. fleet.

Just two minutes later, the course of the whole battle changed when a new wave of 35 U.S. dive-bombers arrived on the scene. The Japanese fighters were all on deck refueling or flying at a low level after shooting down the torpedo-bombers. This was an amazing stroke of luck for the dive-bombers; now they had a clear run at their targets. They swooped down, striking direct hits on *Akagi, Kaga,* and *Soryu,* which were soon in flames and sinking.

The surviving Japanese carrier, the *Hiryu,* launched a successful attack on the *Yorktown,* but it too was then sunk by the U.S. dive-bombers. This meant that the Japanese planes, with nowhere to land, had to crash into the ocean. By evening Japan had lost 332 planes and suffered 2,500 casualties. The Japanese Navy had lost its best-trained pilots and air crews.

Disaster

With his carriers sunk, Yamamoto had to call off the invasion of Midway. This was the first defeat in Japanese naval history. The Japanese people were never told what had happened. Even Prime Minister Tojo was not informed for a whole month. The defeat was partly due to Japanese mistakes, such as Yamamoto's decision to split up his fleet, allowing the United States to fight on equal terms. Still it was a very close call. If the American dive-bombers had arrived just five minutes later, the Japanese fighters would have been ready for them.

Hit by three Japanese bombs and two torpedoes, the Yorktown *tipped over but remained afloat for a day. It was finally sunk by a Japanese submarine.*

CHAPTER SIX

Home Fronts

Home Front United States

The Pacific War was fought not just on the battlefield. Equally important was the ability of factories at home to turn out new ships, planes, tanks, guns, and bombs. Here the United States had an overwhelming advantage. Against Japan's population of 73 million, the United States had a population of 142 million. The country was safe from enemy bombers, rich in raw materials, and already the world leader in industrial production and management.

A young woman inspects artillery shells in one of the new U.S. arms factories.

In 1942 shipbuilder Henry Kaiser began to build aircraft carriers and other war ships in his factories on the West Coast. Kaiser used a workforce of thousands, many of them women, working around the clock. At the beginning of the year, it took six months to build a ship. By September, the workers had grown so efficient that they could do it in just four weeks. The United States was now building ships faster than the Japanese could sink them. This fact alone meant that Japan had no hope of winning the war.

Year	U.S.	JAPAN
1939	5,856	4,467
1940	12,804	4,768
1941	26,277	5,088
1942	47,836	8,861
1943	85,898	16,693
1944	96,318	28,180
1945	49,761	8,263

Between 1939 and 1944, U.S. aircraft production increased dramatically every year. Japan could not hope to keep up.

Unlike the Japanese, the Americans were able to keep improving their planes and weapons. They developed new fast fighter planes and long-range bombers. They invented new weapons, such as the "proximity fuse," a radio transmitter and receiver that caused a shell to explode when it was approaching a target. Thanks to the proximity fuse, U.S. antiaircraft gunners did not have to get a direct hit to shoot down a Japanese plane.

War Films

All governments use propaganda—information that is spread to persuade the public to hold certain opinions. In wartime, government propaganda aims to persuade people that the cause for which they fight is just. With the film industry, based in Hollywood, California, the United States had the best propaganda system in the world. The film studios knew everything about making entertainment for a mass audience, and they offered their services for the war effort. Starting in early 1943, a stream of popular war films poured out of Hollywood, in which stars such as John Wayne and Robert Taylor played brave soldiers killing "devilish" Japanese.

War Movies

Peggy Terry, who worked in a war factory, explained how Hollywood films gave her different attitudes to the Germans and Japanese:

"We understood that the Nazis...would have to be stopped....With the Japanese, that was a whole different thing. We were just ready to wipe them out....They were...creatures that smiled when they bombed our boys....In all the movies we saw... the Germans were good looking and they looked like us. The Japanese were all evil."

Quoted in Studs Terkel, *"The Good War": An American Oral History of World War II*

Home Front Japan

With a tenth of the industries the United States had and a shortage of raw materials, the Japanese had no chance of matching their enemy in war production. Yet they made a desperate effort to keep up. In war factories people worked long hours, often seven days a week. Many of them were women working outside the home for the first time in their lives.

Neighborhood Associations

Japanese people were much more strictly controlled by their government than Americans. Starting in 1940 every Japanese had to join a *tonari-gumi* or "neighborhood association." This was a grouping of ten households under a government-appointed leader. The association had regular meetings where the leader read official announcements and checked on the loyalty of the members.

On December 10, 1941, all the neighborhood associations assembled to listen to a radio broadcast, announcing the outbreak of the war with the United States and its allies. "Every home is a battleground now!" said the announcer. "We are all comrades in arms! Neighborhood love is burning like a flame! Let us sacrifice every bit of our lives for the emperor!"

No Private Life

The Way of the Subject, an official publication of 1941, told Japanese people that they had no right to a private life:

"It is unforgivable to consider private life as the realm of individual freedom where we can do as we like...A meal at table or a suit of clothes, nothing is ours alone... All is related to the concerns of the state. Even in our private lives we should be devoted to the Emperor and never lose our attitude of service to him."

Controlling the News

In times of war, governments routinely attempt to suppress freedom of speech while manipulating the media. Although the United States was no exception, Japan was decidedly more restrictive and controlling of what news its citizens could hear. Radios and newspapers never mentioned any Japanese defeats. People were told that Japan was fighting a just war that had been started by President Roosevelt's cutting off of the country's oil supply. The Japanese were now fighting on behalf of all Asian people to free them from the rule of non-Asians. It was against the law to voice any doubts about the war.

As things began to go badly for Japan, it became harder to make people believe in victory. In the Pacific, U.S. submarines began to sink Japanese merchant ships bringing food and supplies. The hunger that resulted throughout Japan was one fact the government could not deny.

The Japanese public were prepared to make great sacrifices to help the war effort. Here volunteers undertake rail repairs in Osaka.

In a War Factory

Tanara Tetsuko described her life as a teenage girl working in a war factory:

"We were so hungry that we ate our lunch at the same time as our breakfast, since that was so spare. We worked twelve hours straight....We did our best. Our spirit was in it, but whenever we got messages or packages from home we broke down....When the war ended, we felt that all we had done, all that effort, everything we had suffered, had been in vain. I was overwhelmed by a sense of emptiness."

Quoted in Haruko and Theodore Cook, *Japan at War: An Oral History*

In Japan's Empire

The Japanese claimed that they had conquered the empire on behalf of all Asian peoples. Having driven the westerners out, they said, Japan would lead Asia toward prosperity. The empire was called the "Greater East Asia Co-Prosperity Sphere." Japanese soldiers carried banners saying "With firmness we fight. With kindness we build" and "Fight on until Asia is Asia's own." Many Japanese people sincerely believed in these slogans. Others saw them as simply practical, aimed at winning support for Japanese rule. Junsuke Hitomi, who wrote propaganda aimed at Asians, said, "We were trying to think of ways to gain advantage in Asia."

Asian Attitudes

Attitudes toward the Japanese varied from place to place. In the Dutch East Indies (Indonesia) and in Burma, Japanese soldiers were warmly welcomed. Many Indonesian and Burmese people hated their Dutch and British rulers and were delighted to see them thrown

This Japanese leaflet shows British Prime Minister Churchill whipping a blindfolded Indian into battle. The leaflet was aimed at Indian soldiers serving in the British Army.

out. Nogi Harumichi, a Japanese officer, recalled his welcome in the Dutch East Indies: "We Japanese were being treated as liberators [people who set others free]... I felt we were doing something wonderful there." It was very different in the Philippines. The United States had already given these islands the right to self-rule, so the Japanese could not pretend to be liberators. They were not welcome.

Superior Beings

Asians soon found out that the Japanese were even more brutal and arrogant than their former western rulers. The conquerors expected other Asians to bow to them and to make way for them in the streets. Lee Kuan Yew, later to be Prime Minister of Singapore, recalled, "They came in as conquerors and superior beings.... They left nobody in any doubt that they were here for the next thousand years."

In the Dutch East Indies, the Japanese lost people's goodwill by seizing the rice harvest to feed their troops. Millions of Indonesians were then forced to work for the Japanese, mining coal and building railroads and airfields. On forced labor projects, Asians suffered even greater losses than prisoners of war. Alongside the 60,000 prisoners building the Burma-Siam "Death Railroad" (see page 19), there were 300,000 Asians from Java, Malaya, and Burma. Three-quarters of them may have died working on the railroad.

No Asian people suffered more than the Chinese. Because China was at war with Japan, all Chinese people in conquered territory were treated with suspicion. In Singapore, which had a large Chinese population, 50,000 were murdered in the weeks after the city was captured.

Experiments

In mainland China, thousands of Chinese were used in army medical experiments where they were injected with deadly bacteria. The aim was to produce bacteria for use against enemy soldiers. Yoshio Shinozuka, who worked on the experiments, said:

"The easiest way to test the bacteria was on Chinese people, in which process they were killed ... The fact that we called them marutas (logs) shows that we treated them as materials ... I don't think we regarded them as people."

Quoted in Jonathan Lewis and Ben Steele, *Hell in the Pacific*

33

CHAPTER SEVEN

U.S. Offensives

Two months after the Midway victory, the U.S. Navy was ready to launch its first attack of the Pacific War. This was the invasion of Guadalcanal, one of the Solomon Islands northeast of Australia. The Japanese had started building an airfield on Guadalcanal. Once completed it could be used to cut off supply lines to Douglas MacArthur's forces in Australia. Guadalcanal had to be captured.

The Marines

The invasion of Guadalcanal was carried out by marines, soldiers attached to the Navy and trained to fight on land and sea. In the Pacific War, the U.S. Marines specialized in seaborne assaults. They landed from the ocean in enemy-held territory, conquered a "beachhead," and then advanced inland. U.S. Marines prided themselves on being the toughest fighters of the American armed forces. They saw themselves as a band of brothers and had a saying, "Once a marine, always a marine."

A marine on Guadalcanal, armed with a flame thrower, a new weapon used to deadly effect in jungle fighting.

Guadalcanal

At midnight on August 6, 1942, the U.S.
invasion fleet began to pound Guadalcanal
with heavy gunfire. The following morning,
11,000 marines landed on the beaches. They
seized the airfield quickly, because the
Japanese had moved into the jungle to avoid
the bombardment. This was just the
beginning of six months of hard fighting by
land, sea, and air. The Japanese, from their
base at Rabaul, rushed ships to Guadalcanal
and defeated the U.S. Navy in the first of
many battles fought around the island. The
Japanese troops then tried to retake the
airfield, but the marines held on.

On Guadalcanal, the marines had to learn
to fight in the jungle, where the hot damp
air was hard to breathe and they were
constantly bitten by insects. The Japanese

were expert jungle fighters and often attacked at night.
Six days into the campaign, a group of Japanese
soldiers, who said they were wounded and starving,
offered to surrender. It was a trick. Seventeen marines
who went to collect them were ambushed and killed.
Marine Eugene Sledge said, "From then on it was just
intense hatred toward the Japanese...the mentality
[thinking] became "the only good [Japanese] is
a dead [Japanese].'"

These marines in Guadalcanal
are firing a "pack Howitzer,"
a light cannon that could
be taken apart and easily
transported. Ideal for the
jungle, it took just four minutes
to assemble and fire.

Wearing Down

Japan and the United States both sent in reinforcements,
each determined to conquer Guadalcanal. As the months
passed, the campaign became one of attrition, or gradual
wearing down. Victory would go to whichever side could
outlast the other. Japan did not have the resources to win
a campaign of attrition. When their food and medicine
ran out, the hungry and sick Japanese soldiers gave
Guadalcanal a new name— "Starvation Island." In
February 1943, after losing about 24,000 soldiers, the
Japanese finally gave up trying to retake the island.

"Good Hunting"

By 1943 the Japanese had lost the initiative in the war. From now on they would be forced to defend their conquests against the growing U.S. forces. To prepare for this new phase, in April Admiral Yamamoto set off by plane on an inspection tour of the South Pacific islands. Thanks to their ability to decipher Japanese codes, the U.S. Navy learned that Yamamoto would be flying within range of their planes at Guadalcanal. When Pacific commander Admiral Chester Nimitz was given this information, he decided to have Yamamoto assassinated. President Roosevelt agreed to the plan and Nimitz sent the order, adding "Good luck and good hunting."

This Year We Advance

In his first speech of 1943, President Roosevelt announced that the war had entered a new phase:

"The period of our defensive attrition in the Pacific is drawing to a close. Now our aim is to force the Japanese to fight. Last year, we stopped them. This year, we intend to advance."

Annual Message to Congress, January 7, 1943

Government assassinations of military commanders were almost unheard of, but Yamamoto was seen as a special case. He had been responsible for the attack on Pearl Harbor, which Americans saw as a crime. He was the best enemy commander, so his death would damage Japan's fighting ability. It would also come as a great shock to the Japanese public. On April 18, sixteen U.S. fighter planes caught up with Yamamoto and shot his plane out of the sky. His successor, Admiral Koga, said, "There was only one Yamamoto and no one can replace him."

U.S. Disagreements

The difficulty now facing the United States was deciding where in the Pacific to advance. There was a long-standing rivalry between the army and the navy, and the heads of each service had their own ideas about the best way to beat the Japanese. Army General Douglas MacArthur was the highest-ranking commander in the Pacific, and he felt he should have overall command of the war against Japan. He believed that Nimitz's Pacific fleet should be used to back up his army campaigns. MacArthur had one overriding aim in the war: to go back to the Philippines and rescue the 78,000 troops he had left behind there. He had made his famous promise

"I shall return." and considered keeping this promise a matter of honor. Once the Philippines had been retaken, they could be used as a base to bomb Japan.

Naval chief Admiral Ernest King believed that the Pacific War was the navy's business, just as the European war against Germany was an army matter. King thought that MacArthur was putting his personal ambitions before the wider aim of winning the war. He was determined to keep Nimitz's fleet out of MacArthur's control. King and Nimitz wanted to race through the western Pacific, using new fleets of fast aircraft carriers. The marines would seize key island groups, such as the Marianas, which could then be used to strike at Japan itself.

The island campaigns carried out by Admiral Nimitz and General MacArthur. The map also shows the invasion of Okinawa, which took place in 1945.

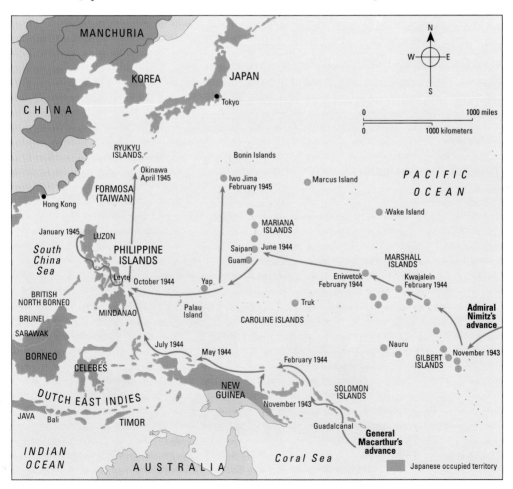

CHAPTER EIGHT

The Island Campaign

After late 1943, Admiral Chester Nimitz's fleet swept up through the western Pacific, making great leaps from one island group to another. The campaign began with the invasion of Tarawa in the Gilbert Islands. The Japanese fiercely defended Tarawa. In three days, 1,100 marines were killed and more than 2,000 wounded. Of almost 5,000 Japanese defenders, only 17 survived to be taken prisoner. At the end the tiny island was covered with dead bodies.

Every battle in the island campaign was just as difficult, with the Japanese defenders always willing to fight to the last man. When they ran out of ammunition, they would rush forward with bamboo spears in mass suicide charges. The marines rarely took Japanese prisoners. Officers said to their men, "It is every Japanese soldier's duty to die for the emperor. It is your duty to see that he does so."

Toward the Marianas

The naval advance caused deep alarm in the Japanese government. By June 1944, the U.S. Navy had reached

Dead soldiers, mostly Japanese, lie on the Tarawa beach. The bodies quickly rotted under the hot tropical sun, and a sickening stench covered the tiny coral island.

the Marianas. These islands were close enough to allow U.S. bombers to strike Japan. Once the bombers arrived, General Tojo knew he could no longer fool the public that Japan was winning the war. To defend the Marianas, the Japanese assembled another great fleet, including nine aircraft carriers with 473 planes. It was commanded by Admiral Jisaburo Ozawa, who was told by his superior, Admiral Soemu Toyoda: "The rise and fall of the Japanese Empire depends on this one battle."

Shooting Turkeys

The Battle of the Philippine Sea on June 19–20, 1944, was the biggest aircraft-carrier battle of the entire war, with fifteen U.S. carriers against Japan's nine. Not surprisingly given these odds, it was another disastrous defeat for Japan. The Japanese pilots, who had had little flying experience, had to fight expert U.S. pilots who had been flying for two years. The Americans also had a new fighter plane, the Hellcat, which was faster and better armed than any Japanese plane. One Hellcat pilot said, "I love this airplane so much...I could marry it." During the first afternoon, the Japanese lost 346 planes to U.S. losses of just 30. The Hellcat pilots found it so easy to shoot down the Japanese that they nicknamed the battle "The Great Marianas Turkey Shoot."

Fall of the Marianas

Once the naval battle had been won, capturing the Marianas was only a matter of time. The battle for Saipan Island proved to be the bloodiest yet, costing the lives of 3,426 marines and 24,000 Japanese soldiers. Thousands of Japanese civilians also killed themselves, throwing themselves from cliff tops into the ocean. The sight of women and children committing suicide in this way shocked even the battle-hardened marines.

The loss of the islands led to the fall of General Tojo's government. This was the first sign that Japan now wanted peace. The problem was that nobody in the new Japanese government knew how to end the war.

On Saipan, two marines try to talk a Japanese soldier into coming out of his hiding place. Thousands preferred suicide to surrender.

MacArthur Returns

While the U.S. Navy raced across the western Pacific, Douglas MacArthur with his U.S. and Australian troops had been slowly moving up the coast of New Guinea toward the Philippines. MacArthur was alarmed at the navy's successes. He dreaded the possibility that his rival, Admiral Nimitz, might win the war before he had the chance to keep his famous promise to return to the Philippines.

Luckily for MacArthur, Nimitz came around to the idea of an invasion of the Philippines for practical reasons. The navy had advanced so quickly across the Pacific that it had become overstretched. Nimitz did not yet have the resources to launch an invasion of his next planned target, Formosa. Rather than slow down his campaign, Nimitz decided to link up with MacArthur and stage a joint invasion of the Philippines.

MacArthur was delighted when he heard this news and amazed when he saw the size of Nimitz's fleet. On October 19, 1944, he stood on the deck of the cruiser *Nashville,* bound for the Philippines. "We have more than 600 ships," MacArthur wrote to his wife." As far as I can see in all directions, there are nothing but ships." The following day MacArthur waded ashore with his

Douglas MacArthur (center) wades ashore at Leyte in the Philippines. He made sure that the photographers were there to record his moment of triumph.

troops on the Philippine island of Leyte. Standing on the beach, he made a dramatic radio broadcast: "People of the Philippines, I have returned!"

Japan's Last Fleet

To defend the Philippines, Admiral Toyoda gathered all his surviving warships into one last great fleet. Toyoda later wrote, "If the worst should happen, there was the risk that we would lose the entire fleet; but I felt that the chance had to be taken … There would be no sense in saving the fleet at the expense of the loss of the Philippines."

After the "Marianas Turkey Shoot," Toyoda did not have enough trained pilots left to fight another air battle. He decided to use his four remaining aircraft carriers as "bait." They would lead the enemy carriers away from the battle area while he used battleships to attack the U.S. landings. Toyoda placed great faith in two huge battleships, the *Yamato* and the *Musashi,* which were the biggest in the world. With armored decks and hulls divided into separate sections, the Japanese believed that these ships were unsinkable.

Battle of Leyte Gulf

From October 23–26, 1944, the rival fleets met in battle around the Philippines. With 282 ships taking part, this was the largest naval battle in history. The Battle of Leyte Gulf was yet another Japanese disaster, thanks to overwhelming U.S. air power. The Japanese lost nine cruisers, eight destroyers, and three battleships. One of these was the "unsinkable" *Musashi,* which was attacked by hundreds of U.S. bomber planes. The aircraft carriers were also sunk. The Imperial Japanese Navy was finished forever.

The U.S. carrier St Lô *explodes during the Battle of Leyte Gulf. A Japanese pilot had deliberately crashed his plane through its flight deck. Half-an-hour later it sank.*

Divine Winds

By October 1944, the United States had won the war at sea and in the air, and it was only a matter of time before Japan was invaded. Vice Admiral Takijiro Onishi, defending the Philippines, came up with a desperate new tactic. His idea was to pack his few remaining planes with bombs and ask his pilots to crash them into the U.S. aircraft carriers. Onishi wrote, "Nothing but the sacrifice of our young men's lives to stab at the enemy's carriers can destroy the enemy fleet and put us on the road to victory."

Before flying to their death, kamikaze pilots often posed for a formal photograph. This was so that their families would remember their courage and self-sacrifice with pride.

Attitudes Toward Dying

On October 24, 1944, Isao Matsuo, a young kamikaze, wrote a last letter to his parents before flying to his death:

"Beloved parents. Please congratulate me. I have been given a splendid opportunity to die. This is my last day ... I shall fall like a blossom from a bright cherry tree. I shall be a shield for the emperor and die cleanly along with my squadron leader and other friends."

Quoted in Raymond Lamont-Brown, *Kamikaze*

Onishi called his suicide pilots "kamikaze" (divine winds). The name referred to two attempts by the Mongol rulers of China to invade Japan in the 13th century. On each occasion, the invasion fleet was scattered by terrible storms. The Japanese believed that these storms were "divine winds" unleashed by the gods to protect Japan. In times of great danger, people said that the gods would again send kamikaze to save the nation.

"It's Hot Today!"

U.S. servicemen were horrified by kamikaze attacks. Naval Lieutenant Frank Manson said, "Every man I believe has a breaking point, and the kamikaze tests that breaking point more than any other form of combat." Manson saw this for himself when a gunner on board his ship, who had spent hours shooting down the kamikazes, suddenly broke down. Unable to bear it any longer, he shouted "It's hot today!" and jumped off the side of the ship to his death.

Results

Between October 1944 and August 1945, 2,940 pilots flew kamikaze missions. Most of them were untrained young men on their first missions, flying outdated planes. These attacks sank 21 U.S. ships and badly damaged 67, with a loss of more than 5,000 Americans killed and the same number wounded. Yet this was too little too late to put Japan "on the road to victory."

Putting On a Brave Face

Kanji Suzuki was a kamikaze who survived after crashing into the sea. Looking back, he explained that he had been afraid of dying but felt that he had to put on a brave face:

"People wanted to become a kamikaze because society respected you, and it was something to be very proud of...When I left home, with much back-slapping and ceremony, I felt like a hero and behaved like one. But once it had all sunk in...I'd feel anxious and scared all day long."

Quoted in Jonathan Lewis and Ben Steele, *Hell in the Pacific*

The Japanese press presented the young pilots as modern-day samurai (Japanese heroic warriors). This pilot on a magazine cover wears a samurai sword.

Hell on Iwo Jima

"If ever hell looked like anything," said one marine, "it must have looked like Iwo Jima." He was talking about a tiny barren island, just 5 miles (8 km) long and 4 miles (6 km) wide, almost 620 miles (1,000 km) south of Japan. At one end is Mount Suribachi, an extinct volcano. All over the island, jets of steam rise through cracks in the rocks and there is a stink of rotten eggs, giving the place its Japanese name, Iwo Jima ("sulphur island").

Decision to Invade

Iwo Jima lies halfway between Japan and the Marianas, where the long-range U.S. bombers were based. From November 1944, these bombers began to attack Japan, flying round trips of 2,400 miles (3,700 km). In December, the U.S. chiefs of staff decided to capture Iwo Jima to provide an emergency landing place for the bombers. The island could also be used by fighter planes, which did not have the range to reach Japan from the Marianas. The fighters would escort the bomber planes, protecting them from enemy aircraft.

Japanese defenses at Iwo Jima. The plan was to let the Americans land on the undefended beaches, and then hit them with a massive bombardment.

Preparations

The Japanese expected Iwo Jima to be invaded, and had spent four months building defenses. An army of 25,000 Japanese soldiers led by General Tadamichi Kuribayashi dug a network of deep tunnels and trenches. Kuribayashi knew that he had no chance of defeating the invasion because there was no Japanese fleet to come to his rescue. His aim was to make the American victory a costly one. Kuribayashi

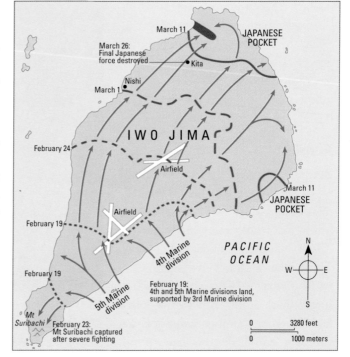

gave the order to his soldiers, "Each man will make it his duty to kill ten of the enemy before dying." The attack on Iwo Jima was planned by U.S. Marine commander General Holland "Howlin' Mad" Smith. He predicted, "This will be the bloodiest fight in Marine Corps history. We'll catch seven kinds of hell on the beaches, and that will be just the beginning."

Hitting the Beach

The invasion was preceded by the longest bombardment of the Pacific War. Beginning in December, the island was attacked for six weeks, day and night, by bomber planes. The battleships arrived on February 15 and, for three days, pounded the island with their big guns. Sheltering deep in their tunnels, the Japanese waited, their fingers pressed in their ears to keep out the noise.

On February 19, 30,000 U.S. Marines climbed down into landing craft and headed for the shore. One marine recalled, "As soon as you got into the boats, you were scared. You were scared until you hit the beach." The Japanese came out of their tunnels and watched the landing craft approach. As soon as they were within range, Kuribayashi gave the order to open fire. As they landed on the beach, the marines found themselves caught in the open under intense Japanese fire. On the first day, 2,500 of them were killed or wounded. Joe Rosenthal, a war photographer, said, "No man who survived that beach can tell you how he did it. It was like walking through rain and not getting wet, and there's no way you can explain it."

Marines take shelter behind a rock while a Japanese shell explodes just a few feet away. Looking at this photograph, you can see why the marines described Iwo Jima as "hell on earth."

Navajos

During the landings on Iwo Jima, different marine units passed on messages and orders by radio. To stop the Japanese from understanding, the messages were read out and received by Native American Navajos in their own language. This language is so complex that it is only understood by Navajos and a handful of other Americans. The Japanese had no idea what the Navajos were saying. Major Howard Connor, marine signal officer, later said, "Were it not for the Navajos, the marines would never have taken Iwo Jima."

Raising the Flag

The marines slowly fought their way inland from the beaches. They met the defenders in hand-to-hand combat, and cleared the tunnels and caves with grenades and flame throwers, weapons that sprayed a long stream of burning oil.

Three of the soldiers who helped raise the U.S. flag on Mount Suribachi were to die on Iwo Jima.

On February 23 a group of marines climbed Mount Suribachi, where six of them raised the Stars and Stripes. Joe Rosenthal's photograph of the flag-raising would become the most famous image of the Pacific War. Watching from below, the marines cheered when they saw the U.S. flag fluttering on the mountain, but they had still only conquered a third of the island.

"Howlin' Mad" Smith expected that it would take him ten days to conquer Iwo Jima. In the end, it took more than five weeks and cost the lives of over 6,000 marines, including three of the men photographed raising the flag. More than 19,000 were wounded. Almost all the Japanese defenders died, including General Kuribayashi. He killed himself in the manner of an ancient Japanese samurai (warrior). Kneeling, he opened his belly with a knife, while an officer cut off his head with a sword.

Marine Bravery

Unlike the Japanese, few marines thought it was their duty to die for their country. Yet they fought just as bravely as the Japanese. On Iwo Jima, seven marines gave their lives to save others by throwing themselves on grenades. Admiral Nimitz later wrote, "Among the Americans who served on Iwo Jima, uncommon valor [bravery] was a common virtue." Looking back, those who served often say that their most important reason for fighting was loyalty to friends. Marine George Peto said, "There were never thoughts about 'I'm doing this for my country'....You're doing it because you're there…you can't leave your buddies and they wouldn't leave you either."

Last Message

On March 18 General Kuribayashi sent a radio message to Japan:

"The gods would weep at the bravery of the officers and men under my command…Our troops with empty hands carried out a series of desperate fights against an enemy possessing overwhelming material superiority…. I regret very much that I have allowed the enemy to occupy a piece of Japanese territory. Now there is no more ammunition. No more water. All the survivors will engage in a general attack."

Quoted in John Toland, *The Rising Sun: The Decline and Fall of the Japanese Empire*

Throughout the battle for Iwo Jima, the U.S. Navy sent in a stream of landing ships with supplies and fresh troops. Here you can see Mount Suribachi in the background.

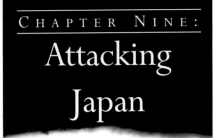

CHAPTER NINE:

Attacking Japan

In November 1944 the U.S. Army Air Force began to attack the Japanese home islands. For these raids, they used the new B-29 "superfortress," the biggest and fastest bomber plane of the war. At first the campaign was aimed at military targets, such as aircraft factories. This was called "precision bombing" and it meant flying during daylight so that the targets could be seen. To avoid Japanese fighter planes and antiaircraft guns, the superfortresses flew at heights of over 30,000 feet (9,000 m). The problem was that strong winds, common at this height, made the planes burn extra fuel and gave the pilots trouble flying. They rarely hit their targets.

New Tactics

In January 1945, Major General Curtis LeMay took over the campaign, and introduced a bold new tactic. Instead of daylight precision bombing, he decided to attack Japan's cities at night with incendiaries – bombs that started fires. LeMay ordered his pilots to fly low, at about 4,500 feet (1,370 m), to avoid the strong winds. Cutting the number of guns and crew in each superfortress allowed more bombs to be carried. Flying low with reduced defenses troubled the pilots until they found that enemy opposition barely existed at night.

LeMay's new tactic meant attacking thickly populated civilian areas rather than military targets. LeMay justified this because many Japanese war industries were spread out in small workshops and homes. The aim was to break the will of the Japanese people and show them that they had lost the war. In 1939 President Roosevelt had condemned the Japanese bombing of Chinese civilians as a crime. By 1945 attitudes had changed. Hatred of the Japanese was now so great that most Americans felt that they deserved every bomb that landed on them.

Tokyo Fire Storm

During the night of March 9, 1945, 302 B-29s attacked Tokyo, dropping almost 500,000 small firebombs. Each bomb contained napalm, a mixture of fuels in sticky jelly. The bombs, scattered over a wide area, stuck to rooftops, starting fires that were impossible to put out. Japanese buildings, made of wood, plaster, and paper, burned easily, and a strong gale fanned the flames. Over a two-hour period, between 80,000 and 100,000 Japanese civilians were, in LeMay's words, "scorched and boiled and baked to death." This was the most destructive conventional air raid in history.

Cities of Fire

The March 9 raid was one of seven big raids on Tokyo. By the end of May, more than half of the capital had been completely destroyed. At the same time, Japan's four other big cities, Kobe, Nagoya, Osaka, and Yokahama, were also devastated. In June, with the big cities in ashes, LeMay turned his bombers loose on 120 smaller cities and towns. There was now no opposition at all from the Japanese. A U.S. pilot recalled that a bombing raid on Japan "was considered to be about the safest pastime a man could enjoy."

"Running For Their Lives"

Hidezo Tsuchikura, a survivor of the fire storm attack on Tokyo, said:

"I watched hundreds of people, adults and children, running for their lives, dashing madly about like rats. The flames raced after them like living things, striking them down."

Quoted in John Costello, *The Pacific War*

This is what Tokyo looked like after just one night raid by Curtis LeMay's superfortresses.

Submarine War

One of the least-known campaigns of the Pacific War was the one carried out beneath the ocean by submarines. Yet this was just as important as LeMay's bombing raids in defeating Japan. Submarines played a big role in destroying the Japanese Imperial Navy, sinking 201 of the 686 warships lost. Even more important was their campaign against merchant shipping. By the end of the war, the Japanese had lost 2,117 merchant vessels, 60 percent of them sunk by submarines.

Japan had gone to war to capture raw materials such as oil and iron. By sinking the merchant fleet, U.S. submarines stopped these materials from reaching Japan's factories. As a result, by the end of the war the Japanese were building planes out of wood and stockpiling bows and arrows instead of guns.

A new U.S. submarine, the Runner, *is launched in June 1942. A year later, it would be destroyed by a Japanese mine, with the loss of all seventy-eight crewmen.*

Life in a Submarine

Submariners lived for weeks in a small, cramped, stuffy space with almost 80 others. A typical vessel had a range of 96,000 miles (16,000 km) and carried supplies for 60 days, the length of the longest possible mission. At sea, the crew seldom washed because they needed to save fresh water.

Life on a submarine was extremely dangerous. On the surface submarines were hunted down by planes, and beneath the ocean by ships using sonar (sound waves). Once found, a submarine would be attacked with "depth charges," bombs dropped into the ocean that exploded when they reached a preset depth. Submarines did not have to be directly hit to be destroyed. Shock waves from an underwater explosion could rip the hull open, and send water pouring inside.

Of the fleet of 288 U.S. submarines, 52 were sunk, killing 3,600 men. Conditions were so dangerous and uncomfortable that all submariners had to be volunteers. The officers preferred thinking for themselves. Out at sea, a submarine captain, unlike a ship's captain, made every decision.

Japanese Submarines

Japan also had a submarine fleet, but used it much less effectively. This was partly because the United States had better equipment for hunting and destroying submarines. From a military point of view, the Japanese also wasted their fleet by using it to carry supplies to the starving soldiers on the Pacific islands. In the last months of the war, Japanese submariners also began to use suicide tactics. They would launch a torpedo called a *kaiten* ("heaven shaker") with a man inside to steer it.

Human torpedoes

Kozu Naoji, who helped launch several kaiten, described what it was like for the men who became "human torpedoes":

"You've already determined your course, peering through the periscope ....You submerge. You run full speed at the estimated enemy position. From the moment you commence your attack, you see nothing....You don't know the moment of your death. You may even die ahead of schedule.... Such a hardhearted weapon!"

Quoted in Haruko and Theodore Cook, *Japan at War: An Oral History*

This is one type of Japanese "human torpedo." It was steered toward an enemy ship by a volunteer wearing a diving suit. Another type, the kaiten, had the volunteer shut inside.

CHAPTER TEN

Atomic Bombs

A Terrible New Weapon

On April 12, 1945, President Roosevelt died suddenly, just as the allies were on the brink of victory over Germany. Harry S. Truman, the vice president, now had the daunting task of replacing Roosevelt as president. Truman learned just how heavy his responsibility was on April 25, when he had a meeting with Harry Stimson, his secretary of war. Stimson announced that U.S. scientists were building "the most terrible weapon ever known in human history." This was an "atomic bomb," a weapon so powerful that just one could destroy a whole city. The bomb would be ready to use by August.

The decision on whether or not to use the new bomb would be the president's alone. After the meeting, Truman said to an aide, "I am going to have to make a decision which no man in history has ever had to make ... It is terrifying to think about what I will have to decide."

Okinawa

When Truman became president, the marines had just begun their invasion of Okinawa, 345 miles (570 km) southwest of Japan. The battle, which lasted from April 1 until June 21, was the bloodiest of the Pacific War. U.S. forces lost 12,613 dead and 40,000 wounded, while more than 110,000 Japanese and Okinawans also died. Following the battle for Okinawa, Truman's military advisers told him that an invasion of Japan itself could cost the lives of a million Americans. Truman, horrified, needed to find a way to end the war without having to invade Japan.

Tired marines rest on the Japanese island of Okinawa shortly after their landing.

Unconditional Surrender

Japan's leaders knew that they had lost the war. In May, after Germany surrendered, they asked the Soviet Union for help in reaching a peace settlement. Their problem was the U.S. demand for unconditional Japanese surrender. This meant that Japan would have to accept any terms the United States imposed. The leaders feared that the U.S. government might remove their emperor and even try him as a war criminal. Prime Minister Zenko Suzuki said, "Should the emperor system be abolished, [Japan] would lose all reason for existence. 'Unconditional surrender'...leaves us no choice but to go on fighting to the last man."

Several of Truman's advisers told him that the Japanese would surrender if they were allowed to keep Emperor Hirohito. Yet Truman felt he could not change his demand for unconditional surrender. He agreed with army chief General Marshall, who said that the demand showed "our people that we were going through with this thing to the finish."

President Harry Truman (left) talks to Secretary of War Henry Stimson two days after the first atomic bomb was dropped on Japan.

Shock Tactics

Truman, Stimson, and Marshall all agreed that atomic bombs would have to be used to force Japan to surrender. Stimson wrote that this would be "a tremendous shock which would carry convincing proof of our power to destroy the Empire." They discussed how to use the bombs and whether the Japanese should be given a warning beforehand. Marshall said, "If you warn them there's no surprise. And the only way to produce shock is surprise." So President Truman decided to drop atomic bombs, without warning, on two Japanese cities.

Impressing the Russians

Truman had another motive for using atomic bombs. He had fallen out with the Soviet leader, Joseph Stalin. Soviet armies now occupied much of Central Europe, and Stalin disagreed with Truman over the future government of the occupied countries. Truman knew that he would soon have to withdraw his own armies from Europe. He hoped to impress Stalin with the power of his terrible new bombs and his willingness to use them. Stalin had already promised to join the United States in its war with Japan. This promise now worried Truman. He wanted to finish the war quickly, before the Soviets joined in the fighting and conquered too much Japanese territory.

Little Boy

In the early morning of August 6, 1945, Lieutenant Colonel Paul Tibbets took off from the Philippines in a B-29 superfortress. His plane, called *Enola Gay* after his mother, carried a single large atomic bomb, nicknamed "Little Boy." Tibbets flew toward the city of Hiroshima. This target had been chosen because it was one of the few Japanese cities that had not yet been devastated by fire raids. The destruction of an undamaged city was the best way of showing the power of the new weapon.

At 8:15 A.M., Major Thomas Ferebee opened the *Enola Gay's* bomb bay doors, and sent "Little Boy" hurtling down toward Hiroshima. Tibbets immediately went into a steep turn, to fly as far away as possible. Fifty-three seconds later, a blinding white flash filled the sky, and the plane was shaken by a massive blast. Tibbets looked down, and saw a rising cloud, forming the shape of a giant mushroom. Below the cloud, Tibbets said that the city now looked like "a boiling pot of tar."

Colonel Paul Tibbets stands in front of his plane, the Enola Gay, *which would carry the bomb to Hiroshima. Looking back in 2001 at his mission, Tibbets said, "I never lost a night's sleep over that."*

Ten square miles (Sixteen sq km) of Hiroshima had been flattened. More than 100,000 Japanese civilians were killed in an instant, many leaving no trace behind except their shadows, imprinted on the ground. Thousands more died later, from wounds and a new disease, "radiation sickness." President Truman was pleased when he heard that the bomb had worked. He said, "This is the greatest thing in history!"

Hiroshima after the dropping of "Little Boy." The city was flattened in seconds.

More Bad News

In Japan, the dropping of the bomb was quickly followed by more bad news. In the early morning of August 8, the Soviet Union declared war on Japan and attacked the Japanese army in Manchuria. For Prime Minister Suzuki, who had hoped that the Soviets might help Japan reach a peace settlement, this was a crushing blow. Suzuki said, "The war must stop immediately."

The next day, the United States dropped a second atomic bomb, on the city of Nagasaki, killing 60,000 to 80,000 more people. The United States only had two atomic bombs. Dropping them so closely together was a way of increasing their shock impact. It gave the impression that the Americans had many bombs and would go on bombing Japanese cities one after another.

CHAPTER ELEVEN

Victory and Defeat

Japan Surrenders

Despite the atomic bombs, the Japanese leaders were still unwilling to agree to unconditional surrender. On August 10, they sent a message that they would surrender, but only if Emperor Hirohito could keep his right to rule. The Americans had already decided to keep Hirohito, but on their terms. They answered that he could continue to be emperor but that he would now have to obey a Supreme Commander appointed by the United States.

When the Japanese leaders could not agree upon the new offer, on August 14 Hirohito summoned them to a meeting in his palace. With tears in his eyes, he ordered his government to accept the terms. "We cannot continue the war any longer," he said. "I cannot let my subjects suffer any longer." At midnight, Hirohito recorded a speech to be broadcast to the Japanese people the next day. With great understatement, he

On the deck of the USS Missouri, General Yoshijuro Umezu signs the Japanese document of surrender, on September 2, 1945. In front of him are Admiral Nimitz, General MacArthur, and representatives of all the allied powers.

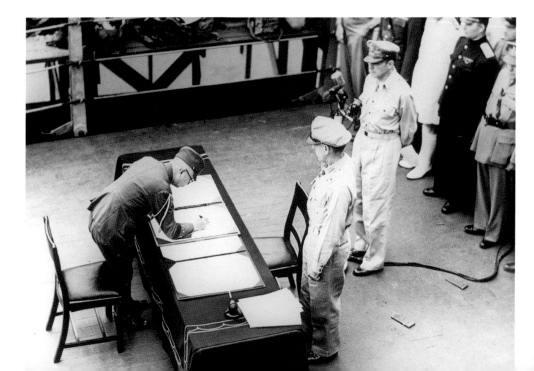

said, "The war situation has developed not necessarily to Japan's advantage." The listeners, most of whom had never heard his voice before, were stunned. For the first time in their history, the Japanese had lost a war.

Attitudes Toward the Bomb

Ever since 1945 people have argued about whether Truman was right to use atomic bombs. Almost all the U.S. military leaders, including Admiral King, Douglas MacArthur, and Curtis LeMay, believed that Japan would have surrendered soon without the bombs. By August they believed that it would not even be necessary to invade Japan.

Admiral William Leahy later wrote, "The use of this barbarous [cruel] weapon was of no material assistance [practical help] in our war against Japan. The Japanese were already defeated and ready to surrender because of our effective sea blockade and the successful bombing with conventional weapons." President Truman never had any doubts that he had made the right decision. He said he had acted "in order to shorten the agony of war, in order to save the lives of thousands and thousands of young Americans." In 1945, most Americans also supported Truman. Every U.S. serviceman in the Pacific rejoiced that the fighting was finally over. Truman had saved their lives.

Japanese prisoners in the Philippines listen to the shocking news that Japan has surrendered.

"They Suffered the Same as We Did"

U.S. Marine Victor Tolley cheered when he heard about the atomic bombings. His attitude changed in September 1945, when he was sent to Nagasaki as part of the occupying army. Tolley made friends with ordinary Japanese citizens and was shocked to discover that they were like human beings everywhere:

"It dawned on me that they suffered the same as we did...I realized that these people didn't want to fight us. What the military did and what the civilians did were two different things ....We didn't drop those [bombs] on military installations. We dropped them on women and children ...75,000 human beings that lived and breathed and ate and wanted to live that were in an instant charred."

Quoted in Studs Terkel, *"The Good War": An American Oral History of World War II*

Making Peace

On August 30, 1945, General Douglas MacArthur landed by plane in Japan, like a conquering hero. He was the Supreme Commander appointed by Truman, who would rule Japan for the next six years. He commanded an occupying army of 250,000 American soldiers.

Remaking Japan

MacArthur had the task of remaking Japan as an American-style democracy. With a team of experts, he drew up a new constitution—a document outlining Japan's future government. This gave many new rights to Japanese people. In the future, Japan would be ruled by leaders elected by the people. For the first time, women could vote, enter parliament, own property, divorce their husbands, and have a higher education. The constitution also declared that Japan had given up warfare for all time, and would no longer maintain any armed forces. Emperor Hirohito was to be kept on as a figurehead, though he publicly announced that he should no longer be thought of as a god.

Japan was purged of militarists. Anybody suspected of supporting militarism could no longer play a role in public life. In all, 210,288 Japanese people were fired, including professors, teachers, newspaper editors, police chiefs, and politicians. Trials of war criminals were also held: 984 Japanese were hanged and 4,405 imprisoned.

Tojo on Trial

The most famous trial was of General Tojo and 27 other Japanese leaders, who were charged with the crime of plotting to start the war. This did not go the way that the United States had planned. Tojo argued strongly that his government had acted only in self-defense. Although he was found guilty and hanged, many Japanese people admired the dignified way he stood up to his accusers. One Japanese, quoted in *Time* magazine, said, "I used to think Tojo should be hanged. Now I don't know. If we had won we would have tried the Americans."

Political freedom brought new conflicts for Japanese society. This is a 1946 demonstration against the newly elected Japanese government. Such protest were unheard of before the war.

Winners and Losers

World War II caused destruction and death on a scale previously unknown in history. At its conclusion, almost all the countries involved had bombed-out cities and shattered economies. The exception was the United States, which came out of the war richer and more powerful than ever. Americans used their wealth to help both allies and former enemies rebuild their countries. One reason for doing this was to check the spread of Soviet communism. A new struggle, the "Cold War," had begun between the United States and the Soviet Union. Japan would be a valuable ally to the Americans.

The Japanese leaders had mistakenly believed that a nation had to conquer an empire to be successful. In fact, the age of empires was passing. As a result of the Pacific War the "European empires" in Asia were all destroyed. Asian countries would now have the right to rule themselves. Freed from military spending, Japan could concentrate on producing things that people actually wanted, such as cars and electronic goods. In the second half of the 20th century, Japan developed one of the world's strongest economies.

A Japanese flag displayed alongside the Stars and Stripes in Washington, D.C., in honor of a 1981 visit by the Japanese Prime Minister Zenko Suzuki. The old enemies are now strong allies.

Date List

1931 **September 18** Japanese army invades Manchuria.

1933 **February 21** Japan leaves League of Nations.

1937 **July 7** Japanese begin full-scale war with China.

1939 **September 1** Germany invades Poland.
September 1 Soviet Union invades Poland from the east.
September 3 Britain and France declare war on Germany.

1940 **May 10** Germany conquers Netherlands and Belgium and invades France.
September 13 Japanese occupy northern French IndoChina.

1941 **April 13** Japan and Russia Sign Non-Aggression Pact.
June 22 Germany invades the Soviet Union.
July 26 United States freezes all Japan's assets.
July 28 Japanese occupy southern half of French Indochina.
October 17 General Hideki Tojo becomes Japanese Prime Minister.
December 7-8 Japanese attack Pearl Harbor, Malaya, the Philippines, Singapore, and Hong Kong. (Hawaii is on the other side of the international date line—it was December 7 in Pearl Harbor, but December 8 where the other attacks occurred.)

December 8 United States and Britain declare war on Japan.
December 10 Japanese take Guam in the Philippines. Japanese bombers sink the British battleship *Prince of Wales* and the battle cruiser *Repulse* in waters off Malaya.
December 11 Germany declares war on the United States.
December 23 Japanese capture Wake Island.
December 25 Japanese seize Hong Kong.

1942 **January 2** Manila, the capital of the Philippines, falls to Japan.
January 3 Japanese invade Borneo.
January 11 Japanese invade the Dutch East Indies.
January 15 Japanese invade Burma.
January 23 Japanese invade New Guinea and the Solomon Islands.
February 15 British surrender in Singapore.
February 27–29 Japanese Navy defeats allies in the Battle of the Java Sea.
March 8 Dutch forces in the East Indies surrender to Japan.
March 11 General Douglas MacArthur leaves the Philippines for Australia.
April 9 U.S. and Philippine army surrenders in Bataan.
April 18 The U.S. "Doolittle raid" on Tokyo.
May 4–8 The Battle of the Coral Sea.
June 4–6 U.S. Navy wins the Battle of Midway, the turning point of the war.

August 7 U.S. Marines land on Guadalcanal and begin a six-month campaign.

1943 **February 2** German army surrenders at Stalingrad in the Soviet Union.
February 7–9 Japanese abandon attempt to retake Guadalcanal.
April 18 Admiral Yamamoto's plane is shot down.
June 9-10 British and U.S. armies invade Sicily.
June 29 MacArthur's troops land in New Guinea.
November 20 U.S. Marines land at Tarawa in the Gilbert Islands.

1944 **January 31–February 21** Marines capture the Marshall Islands.
June 6 D-Day: Allied armies land in Normandy, France.
June 15 Marines invade Saipan in the Marianas. First B-29 raid on Japan.
June 19-20 U.S. Navy wins the Battle of the Philippine Sea.
July 18 General Tojo resigns as Japanese Prime Minister.
October 20 Douglas MacArthur lands at Leyte in the Philippines.
October 23–26 Japanese fleet is destroyed in the Battle of Leyte Gulf.

1945 **January 17** Soviets capture the Polish capital, Warsaw.
February 19 U.S. Marines land on Iwo Jima.
March 3 Douglas MacArthur retakes Manila.

March 7 U.S. army crosses the Rhine, into Germany.
March 9–10 Huge fire-bombing raid on Tokyo.
April 1 Marines land in Okinawa.
April 6 Mass kamikaze attacks on U.S. invasion fleet at Okinawa.
April 12 President Roosevelt dies. Harry S. Truman becomes president.
April 30 As the Soviets sweep through Berlin, Adolf Hitler kills himself.
May 7 Germany surrenders.
July 26 Meeting at Potsdam in Germany, the allies demand unconditional Japanese surrender.
August 6 United States drops first atomic bomb on Hiroshima.
August 8 Soviet Union declares war on Japan and invades Manchuria.
August 9 United States drops second atomic bomb on Nagasaki.
August 14 Emperor Hirohito orders his government to surrender.
August 15 Hirohito broadcasts news of the Japanese surrender.
September 2 Douglas MacArthur receives formal Japanese surrender in Tokyo Bay.

1948 **December 23** General Tojo and six other Japanese wartime leaders are hanged.

1951 **September 8** U.S. occupation of Japan ends.

Glossary

aircraft carrier a naval ship with a wide, flat deck, used for launching and recovering aircraft.

antiaircraft guns guns on land, or on ships, aimed at the sky to shoot down planes.

army land fighting force.

atomic bomb a bomb that releases energy that is usually locked up inside the nuclei (center) of atoms of uranium or plutonium. Enormous energy is released when the nuclei are split apart.

attrition gradual wearing down. In a campaign of attrition, victory goes to the side that can outlast the other.

battle cruiser a warship, nearly as large as a battleship, but with thinner armor and smaller guns to make it faster.

battleship the largest type of warship, with the heaviest guns and armor.

blockade surrounding a place to stop supplies from getting through. Naval blockades use ships and submarines to starve an island of food and supplies.

campaign a series of military operations, linked together with a common aim.

casualty in military terms, any fighter killed, wounded, or missing.

Cold War the long conflict between the United States and the Soviet Union that began at the end of World War II. The superpowers fought indirectly, backing different sides in wars around the world. It was called a "cold" war to distinguish it from a "hot," or openly fought, war, such as World War II.

cruiser a fast, medium-sized warship with medium weaponry and armor. Often used to guard convoys (groups of merchant ships sailing together under naval protection).

depth charge a bomb dropped into the ocean, preset to explode at a certain depth, used to destroy submarines.

democracy government by the people. In modern democracies, the people choose their rulers in elections.

destroyer a small, fast warship armed with guns, torpedoes, and depth charges. Its role is to protect fleets by destroying submarines and other small enemy ships.

dive-bomber a fast plane armed with bombs and machine guns, used to attack targets on the ground or at sea.

dysentery a disease of the intestines. Symptoms include painful diarrhea and passing of blood. Dysentery is caused by bacteria in water or food.

economy the way in which a country produces and manages wealth.

fighter plane a small, fast plane armed with machine guns, used to attack other planes.

Great Depression the name given to the world economic crisis of the early 1930s, characterized by mass unemployment and a collapse in international trading.

heavy bomber a large bomber plane, heavily armored and able to fly long distances.

incendiary a bomb that starts fires.

kaiten "heaven shaker," a Japanese torpedo steered by a person inside, who chooses a course by looking through a periscope. This was a suicide weapon.

kamikaze "divine wind," the name for a suicide attack by a Japanese pilot, who would crash his plane into an enemy ship.

malaria a disease passed on by mosquito bites. Its symptoms include a high fever.

Malaya present-day Malaysia.

Marines troops in the navy, trained to fight on land and at sea.

merchant ships ships used to carry goods for trade.

militarists people who want to increase the strength of the armed forces. Militarists are strong believers in "military values" such as discipline and courage.

Navy military ships and crews, and the planes and troops they carry.

Nazi Party German political party led by Adolf Hitler. The name is short for "National Socialist."

New Deal the name of the political program of U.S. president Franklin Roosevelt, intended to solve the economic problems caused by the Great Depression of the 1930s. Roosevelt's goals were to create jobs for the unemployed, to guarantee decent living standards, and to prevent future crises.

periscope a viewing tube fitted with mirrors, allowing people under the ocean in submarines to see ships on the surface.

propaganda information or ideas spread to persuade or influence people.

Sources and Resources

radar a system using radio waves to locate and track distant objects, such as ships and planes. The name comes from radio detection and ranging.

sonar the use of sound waves traveling through water to locate ships or submarines. The sound wave hits the object and bounces back as an echo. The time this takes shows how far away the object is. The name comes from sound detection and ranging.

strategy overall plan of action. Also the management of armed forces during a campaign.

submarine a vessel able to travel under water, used to attack ships on the surface.

suicide deliberate killing of oneself.

superpatriotic patriots are people who are devoted to their country. "Superpatriotic" means taking this devotion to extreme lengths.

tactics a word similar to strategy, but with the narrower meaning of the management of armed forces in actual contact with the enemy.

tonari-gumi ("neighborhood association") a grouping of Japanese households, used by the government to control the public.

torpedo a powered missile that travels through water.

torpedo bomber a plane armed with torpedoes. Torpedo bombers are used to attack enemy ships and submarines and are low flying so they can launch torpedoes in the water.

Further Reading

Aaseng, Nathan. *Navajo Code Talkers*. New York: Walker, 2002.

Bix, Herbert P. *Hirohito and the Making of Modern Japan.*Collingdale, Penn.: DIANE Publishing, 2002.

Cook, Haruko and Theodore. *Japan at War: An Oral History*. Irvine, Calif.: Phoenix Press, 2000.

Gaines, Anne Graham. *Douglas MacArthur: Brilliant General, Controversial Leader.* Berkeley Heights, N.J.: Enslow, 2001.

Newcomb, Richard F. *Iwo Jima: The Dramatic Account of the Epic Battle That Turned the Tide of World War II.* New York: Henry Holt, 2002.

Terkel, Studs. *"The Good War": An American Oral History of World War II*. Irvine, Calif.: Phoenix Press, 2001.

Toland, John. *The Rising Sun: The Decline and Fall of the Japanese Empire*. New York: Penguin Books, 2001.

Index

If a number is in **bold** type, there is an illustration.